Contents

INTRODUCTION 2
CHAPTER ONE 5
   Gastroparesis 5
   Symptoms 6
   Causes 6
   Risk factors 7
   Complications 8
   Diagnosis 9
   Treatment 11
   Changes to your diet 11
   Medications 15
   Surgical treatment 16
   Lifestyle and home remedies 17
   The Three-Phased Diet Approach 21
   Essential Long-Term Diet Tips 23
   Sample Gastroparesis Diet Plan 25
   Sample 3-Day Diet Plan 26
   Gastroparesis and the Low FODMAP Diet 28
CHAPTER TWO 30
   Recipes 30
CONCLUSION 97

INTRODUCTION

Gastroparesis is a condition in which your stomach empties into your small intestine more slowly than it should.

Gastroparesis can be triggered by an illness or a long-term disease, such as diabetes or lupus. Symptoms may be mild or severe, and usually includes vomiting, bloating, nausea, and heartburn.

Sometimes gastroparesis is a temporary sign that your body has something else that you're dealing with. Sometimes it's a chronic, or long-term, condition.

Gastroparesis can also occur after bariatric surgery or another medical procedure that interrupts your digestion.

When you have gastroparesis, the amount of fats and fiber that you eat can greatly affect how intense your symptoms are. Dietary adjustments are sometimes the first method of treatment suggested to people who have gastroparesis.

If you have gastroparesis, it's important to focus on getting the nutrition that you need while eating small, frequent meals that are low in fat and easy to digest. The staples of this kind of diet include high-protein foods (such as eggs and nut butter) and easy-to-digest vegetables (such as cooked zucchini).

If the food is easy to chew and swallow, that's a good indication that you'll have an easier time digesting it. If you currently have gastroparesis symptoms, you should be aware of what foods to avoid.

As a general rule, foods that are high in saturated fat or fiber should only be eaten in small amounts.

When you have gastroparesis, you should be mindful of how often and in what order you consume foods. It's recommended you eat small meals, five to eight times per day.

Chew your food well before swallowing it. Eat nutritious foods first to keep from becoming full from foods that don't fuel your body.

While recovering from gastroparesis, consider taking a multivitamin supplement so that you can still get the nutrition you need. If weight loss has been a symptom of your gastroparesis, aim for a minimum of 1,500 calories a day as you begin your recovery.

CHAPTER ONE

Gastroparesis

Gastroparesis is a condition that affects the normal spontaneous movement of the muscles (motility) in your stomach. Ordinarily, strong muscular contractions propel food through your digestive tract. But if you have gastroparesis, your stomach's motility is slowed down or doesn't work at all, preventing your stomach from emptying properly.

Certain medications, such as opioid pain relievers, some antidepressants, and high blood pressure and allergy medications, can lead to slow gastric emptying and cause similar symptoms. For people who already have gastroparesis, these medications may make their condition worse.

Gastroparesis can interfere with normal digestion, cause nausea and vomiting, and cause problems with blood sugar levels and nutrition. The cause of gastroparesis is usually unknown. Sometimes it's a complication of diabetes, and some people develop gastroparesis after surgery. Although there's no cure for gastroparesis, changes to your diet, along with medication, can offer some relief.

Symptoms

Signs and symptoms of gastroparesis include:
- Vomiting
- Nausea
- A feeling of fullness after eating just a few bites
- Vomiting undigested food eaten a few hours earlier
- Acid reflux
- Abdominal bloating
- Abdominal pain
- Changes in blood sugar levels
- Lack of appetite
- Weight loss and malnutrition

Many people with gastroparesis don't have any noticeable signs and symptoms.

Causes

It's not always clear what leads to gastroparesis. But in many cases, gastroparesis is believed to be caused by damage to a nerve that controls the stomach muscles (vagus nerve).

The vagus nerve helps manage the complex processes in your digestive tract, including signaling the muscles in your stomach to contract and push food into the small intestine. A damaged vagus nerve can't send signals normally to your stomach muscles. This may cause food to remain in your stomach longer, rather than move normally into your small intestine to be digested.

The vagus nerve can be damaged by diseases, such as diabetes, or by surgery to the stomach or small intestine.

Risk factors

- Factors that can increase your risk of gastroparesis:
- Diabetes
- Abdominal or esophageal surgery
- Infection, usually a virus

- Certain medications that slow the rate of stomach emptying, such as narcotic pain medications
- Scleroderma (a connective tissue disease)
- Nervous system diseases, such as Parkinson's disease or multiple sclerosis
- Hypothyroidism (low thyroid)

Women are more likely to develop gastroparesis than are men.

Complications

Gastroparesis can cause several complications, such as:

- Severe dehydration. Ongoing vomiting can cause dehydration.
- Malnutrition. Poor appetite can mean you don't take in enough calories, or you may be unable to absorb enough nutrients due to vomiting.
- Undigested food that hardens and remains in your stomach. Undigested food in your stomach can harden into a solid mass called a bezoar. Bezoars can cause nausea and

vomiting and may be life-threatening if they prevent food from passing into your small intestine.
- Unpredictable blood sugar changes. Although gastroparesis doesn't cause diabetes, frequent changes in the rate and amount of food passing into the small bowel can cause erratic changes in blood sugar levels. These variations in blood sugar make diabetes worse. In turn, poor control of blood sugar levels makes gastroparesis worse.
- Decreased quality of life. An acute flare-up of symptoms can make it difficult to work and keep up with other responsibilities.

Diagnosis

Doctors use several tests to help diagnose gastroparesis and rule out conditions that may cause similar symptoms. Tests may include:
- Gastric emptying study. This is the most important test used in making a diagnosis of gastroparesis. It involves eating a light meal,

such as eggs and toast, that contains a small amount of radioactive material. A scanner that detects the movement of the radioactive material is placed over your abdomen to monitor the rate at which food leaves your stomach.

- You'll need to stop taking any medications that could slow gastric emptying. Ask your doctor if any of your medications might slow your digestion.
- Upper gastrointestinal (GI) endoscopy. This procedure is used to visually examine your upper digestive system — your esophagus, stomach and beginning of the small intestine (duodenum) — with a tiny camera on the end of a long, flexible tube. This test can also diagnose other conditions, such as peptic ulcer disease or pyloric stenosis, which can have symptoms similar to those of gastroparesis.
- Ultrasound. This test uses high-frequency sound waves to produce images of structures

within your body. Ultrasound can help diagnose whether problems with your gallbladder or your kidneys could be causing your symptoms.
- Upper gastrointestinal series. This is a series of X-rays in which you drink a white, chalky liquid (barium) that coats the digestive system to help abnormalities show up.

Treatment

Treating gastroparesis begins with identifying and treating the underlying condition. If diabetes is causing your gastroparesis, your doctor can work with you to help you control it.

Changes to your diet

Maintaining adequate nutrition is the most important goal in the treatment of gastroparesis. Many people can manage gastroparesis with diet changes and dietary changes are the first step in managing this condition. Your doctor may refer you to a dietitian who can work with you to find foods that are easier for you to digest so that you're more likely to get enough calories and nutrients from the food you eat. A dietitian might suggest that you try to:

- Eat smaller meals more frequently
- Chew food thoroughly
- Eat well-cooked fruits and vegetables rather than raw fruits and vegetables
- Avoid fibrous fruits and vegetables, such as oranges and broccoli, which may cause bezoars
- Choose mostly low-fat foods, but if you can tolerate them, add small servings of fatty foods to your diet
- Try soups and pureed foods if liquids are easier for you to swallow
- Drink about 34 to 51 ounces (1 to 1.5 liters) of water a day
- Exercise gently after you eat, such as going for a walk
- Avoid carbonated drinks, alcohol and smoking
- Try to avoid lying down for 2 hours after a meal

- Take a multivitamin daily

Here's a brief list of foods recommended for people with gastroparesis (your dietitian can give you a more comprehensive list):

Starches
- White bread and rolls and "light" whole-wheat bread without nuts or seeds
- Plain or egg bagels
- English muffins
- Flour or corn tortillas
- Pancakes
- Puffed wheat and rice cereals
- Cream of wheat or rice
- White crackers
- Potatoes, white or sweet (no skin)
- Baked french fries
- Rice
- Pasta

Protein
- Lean beef, veal and pork (not fried)
- Chicken or turkey (no skin and not fried)

- Crab, lobster, shrimp, clams, scallops, oysters
- Tuna (packed in water)
- Cottage cheese
- Eggs
- Tofu
- Strained meat baby food

Fruits and vegetables

- Baby food vegetables and fruits
- Tomato sauce, paste, puree, juice
- Carrots (cooked)
- Beets (cooked)
- Mushrooms (cooked)
- Vegetable juice
- Vegetable broth
- Fruit juices and drinks
- Applesauce
- Bananas
- Peaches and pears (canned)

Dairy

- Milk, if tolerated
- Yogurt (without fruit pieces)

- Custard and pudding
- Frozen yogurt

Medications

Medications to treat gastroparesis may include:

- Medications to stimulate the stomach muscles. These medications include metoclopramide (Reglan) and erythromycin (Eryc, E.E.S.). Metoclopramide has a risk of serious side effects. Erythromycin may lose its effectiveness over time, and can cause side effects, such as diarrhea.
- A newer medication, domperidone, with fewer side effects, is also available with restricted access.
- Medications to control nausea and vomiting. Drugs that help ease nausea and vomiting include prochlorperazine (Compro) and diphenhydramine (Benadryl, Unisom). A class of medications that includes ondansetron (Zofran) is sometimes used to help nausea and vomiting.

Surgical treatment

Some people with gastroparesis may be unable to tolerate any food or liquids. In these situations, doctors may recommend a feeding tube (jejunostomy tube) be placed in the small intestine. Or doctors may recommend a gastric venting tube to help relieve pressure from gastric contents.

Feeding tubes can be passed through your nose or mouth or directly into your small intestine through your skin. The tube is usually temporary and is only used when gastroparesis is severe or when blood sugar levels can't be controlled by any other method. Some people may require an IV (parenteral) feeding tube that goes directly into a vein in the chest.

Treatments under investigation

Researchers are continuing to investigate new medications to treat gastroparesis.

One example is a new drug in development called relamorelin. The results of a phase 2 clinical trial found the drug could speed up gastric emptying and reduce vomiting. The drug is not yet approved by the

Food and Drug Administration (FDA), but a larger clinical trial is currently underway.

A number of new therapies are being tried with the help of endoscopy — a slender tube that's threaded down the esophagus. One procedure used endoscopy to place a small tube (stent) where the stomach connects to the small intestine (duodenum) to keep this connection open.

Several research trials investigated the use of botulinum toxin administered through endoscopy without much success. This treatment is not recommended.

Doctors are also studying the use of a minimally invasive surgical technique when someone needs a feeding tube placed directly into the small intestine (jejunostomy tube).

Lifestyle and home remedies

If you're a smoker, stop. Your gastroparesis symptoms are less likely to improve over time if you keep smoking.

People with gastroparesis who are overweight are also less likely to get better over time.

Alternative medicine

There is some evidence that certain alternative treatments can be helpful to people with gastroparesis, although more studies are needed. Some treatments that look promising include:

- Acupuncture and electroacupuncture. Acupuncture involves the insertion of extremely thin needles through your skin at strategic points on your body. During electroacupuncture, a small electrical current is passed through the needles. Studies have shown these treatments to ease gastroparesis symptoms more than a sham treatment.
- STW 5 (Iberogast). This herbal formula from Germany contains nine different herbal extracts. It hasn't been shown to speed up gastric emptying, but was slightly better at easing digestive symptoms than a placebo.
- Rikkunshito. This Japanese herbal formula also contains nine herbs. It may help reduce

abdominal pain and the feeling of post-meal fullness.
- Cannabis. There aren't any published clinical trials on cannabis and gastroparesis. However, cannabis — commonly known as marijuana — is thought to ease nausea and other digestive complaints. Derivatives of cannabis have been used by people who have cancer in the past, but there are better FDA-approved medications available to control nausea now.

Because cannabis is often smoked, there's concern about possible addiction and harm, similar to what occurs with tobacco smoke.

In addition, daily users of marijuana (cannabis) may develop a condition that mimics the symptoms of gastroparesis called cannabis hyperemesis syndrome. Symptoms can include nausea, vomiting and abdominal pain. Quitting cannabis may help.

Best Diet for Gastroparesis

While there is no one best diet for gastroparesis, there are specific strategies that help support digestion and stomach motility.

These four factors impact stomach emptying rate and should be considered when developing a diet for gastroparesis:

- Liquids: Thin liquids like water, broth and juices rapidly empty the stomach. They require little to no digestion and use the effect of gravity to move down to the small intestine. Thicker liquids such as pureed soups or smoothies empty at a slower rate.
- Solids: Solid food requires more work for the stomach, which needs to break it down to pass into the small intestine. This process slows stomach emptying.
- Nutrient Composition: Fiber and fat-rich foods and oils also take longer to empty from the stomach. Carbohydrates can pass through the quickest, followed by proteins.
- Food Temperature: The temperature of food when it enters the stomach affects when it

leaves. Hot meals and beverages will exit the stomach faster than cool foods and liquids.

The Three-Phased Diet Approach

With these concepts in mind, a three-phased diet approach is often recommended for those with gastroparesis.

1 – Phase One:

- Lasting less than three days, the first phase consists of thin liquids and saltine crackers.
- Calories are inadequate, typically under 800 daily, so this phase should last no longer than three days, unless additional nutrition support is included.
- Gatorade, ginger ale and other sodas, broths, juices and water are consumed. Since you'll only be meeting your fluid and electrolyte needs these days, it's important to follow this phase under the supervision of your healthcare provider.

2 – Phase Two:

Fat intake progressively increases up to 40 grams daily. Calories may still be less than adequate, but should slowly increase as tolerated.

- This phase typically lasts 4-6 weeks, but depends on the degree of improvement in your symptoms.
- Food choices may include fat-free dairy, thicker soups, grains (not whole grains), eggs, peanut butter (limit to two tablespoons), fruit and vegetable juices, canned fruits, peeled and well-cooked veggies, and low-fat desserts (puddings, frozen yogurt, gelatin, popsicles, etc.).

3 – Phase Three:

- Calorie and fat intake increases up to 50 grams daily.
- This is considered a maintenance phase, and should still be monitored and modified under the care of your healthcare professional.
- Continue focusing on a low-fiber diet and eating smaller meals spaced throughout the

day. Tailor the diet to meet your specific nutritional needs.

In case your needs are not fully met on this plan, talk to your healthcare provider about using a multivitamin or mineral supplement. In severe cases, short- or long-term enteral (feeding-tube) or parenteral (intravenous) nutrition may be required.

Essential Long-Term Diet Tips

Try these simple diet tips to keep symptoms of gastroparesis at bay:

- Eat Small, Frequent Meals: This allows you to meet your calorie and nutrient needs without overfilling the stomach. You'll feel less bloated and uncomfortable with smaller portions of food.
- Chew Your Food Well: This will help relieve your stomach from overworking to break down food. When food is broken down by your teeth it also has time to mix with salivary enzymes to "pre-digest" before being swallowed.

- Take Advantage of Gravity: By remaining upright and going for a light walk after eating, your food is more likely to be pulled down into the small intestine to continue digesting. Avoid eating too late at night and/or taking naps or reclining in a chair after eating.
- Consider Liquid-Meal Replacements: Products like Ensure and Boost or homemade protein shakes or smoothies can help you meet your calorie needs.
- Avoid High-Fat Foods: Skip the fried foods, high-fat meats, full-fat dairy and baked goods. Instead, enjoy limited amounts of healthy fats like extra virgin olive oil, avocado, nut or seed butters and fatty fish.
- Limit Fiber Intake: Avoid high fiber foods like whole grains and legumes (e.g. beans, peas, lentils), as well as the skins and seeds of fruits and veggies. This helps reduce the risk of developing bezoars, which can cause stomach blockages.

- Enjoy Your Nuts & Seeds Pureed: Nut and seed butters are more easily digested than whole nuts and seeds. But don't overdo these if you're trying to lose weight— they're still high in fat and therefore high in calories.
- Choose Nutrient-Dense Foods: Since every calorie counts, don't waste them on junk food. Choose 100% juice, low-fat dairy products (e.g. yogurt, cheese, milk), peeled fruits and vegetables, lean meats and seafood. Occasional intake of treats is okay, focusing on lower fat options like rice krispy treats, low fat pudding and angel food cake.
- Avoid Alcoholic Spirits: Drinks like vodka, rum, tequila, etc., can slow gastric motility.
- Summary: While there's not one best diet for gastroparesis, you should aim to eat slowly and enjoy small frequent meals. You must also choose nutrient-rich foods that are low in fat and fiber.

Sample Gastroparesis Diet Plan

Your maintenance diet for gastroparesis may include the following foods:

- Fruits & Vegetables: baby food, homemade fruit and vegetable purees, canned and/or frozen fruits and vegetables, 100% fruit or vegetable juice, smoothies, pureed low-fat vegetable soups, well-cooked and de-skinned vegetable
- Proteins: low-fat or fat-free milk, low-fat or fat-free yogurt, low-fat or fat-free cheese, lean (not skin, fat-trimmed) meat and poultry, ground lean meats, eggs or egg whites, fish, shellfish, limited creamy nut/seed butters
- Starches: white rices, white breads, mashed potatoes (skin removed), pastas, noodles, crackers, cereals (avoid whole grains)
- Oils: any as long as they are limited overall (under 50 grams of fat daily)

Sample 3-Day Diet Plan

Below is a sample meal plan you may follow, though it should be adjusted for your specific calorie and nutrient needs.

Day One:
- Breakfast: 1 cup of puffed rice cereal with skim milk and sliced ripe bananas
- Snack 1: apple sauce
- Lunch: chicken noodle soup, 6 saltine crackers
- Snack 2: saltine crackers with a thin layer of almond butter
- Dinner: Chinese stir fry with white rice, tofu, well-cooked veggies (carrots, onions, snow peas) with soy sauce
- Snack 3: low-fat pudding cup

Day Two:
- Breakfast: 2 slices of white toast lightly topped with peanut butter and strawberry jam, Ensure/Boost shake
- Snack 1: canned peaches
- Lunch: egg noodles tossed with steamed shrimp and stewed tomatoes
- Snack 2: green juice, pretzels
- Dinner: roasted vegetable soup, side of turkey

- Snack 3: frozen yogurt popsicle

Day Three:
- Breakfast: scrambled egg whites with sauteed spinach and pinch of low-fat cheddar cheese, side of canned pineapple chunks
- Snack 1: protein shake
- Lunch: smoothie with low-fat yogurt, frozen berries, orange juice, protein powder
- Snack 2: vegetable soup
- Dinner: baked salmon with side of mashed potatoes
- Snack 3: cream of wheat with honey and spoonful of peanut butter

Gastroparesis and the Low FODMAP Diet

If you have implemented all the above strategies with little success, there is one other option.

The main symptoms of gastroparesis (particularly bloating) greatly overlap with those of irritable bowel syndrome (IBS) and small intestinal bacterial overgrowth(SIBO). Both these conditions can be treated with a low FODMAP diet, among other things.

In fact, there is evidence that those with gastroparesis are much more likely to have or develop SIBO.

Given the overlap, some doctors and even patients have begun to wonder if minimizing FODMAPs will also help with this condition. I was unable to find any scientific literature yet, but theoretically it makes sense that it would help.

Diet Changes Requires Some Trial and Error

Gastroparesis slows down the rate at which food in the stomach empties.

It's often due to conditions that impair the nerve and muscle functioning of the stomach. While medical treatments are available, dietary change is the initial and ideal option.

The best diet for gastroparesis typically depends on the severity of the condition. Initially you may consider trying the three-phased gastroparesis diet, which starts with clear liquids, and then slowly progresses to a maintenance plan of nutrient-rich foods.

When symptoms are acting up, it's generally best to eat smaller meals, limit fiber, choose low-fat options and consider liquid meal replacements as needed. You can also consider trialling a low FODMAP diet if nothing else has helped. Making these simple changes to the way you eat can go a long way to successfully managing gastroparesis.

CHAPTER TWO

Recipes

Here are some recipes to try on a gastroparesis diet

Tagliatelle With Prosciutto and Peas

INGREDIENTS

- 1 lb. tagliatelle
- 1½ cups shelled fresh peas (from about 1½ lb. pods) or frozen peas

- ½ cup (1 stick) unsalted butter
- 6 oz. prosciutto, thinly sliced (about 12 slices)
- 16 sage leaves
- 2 oz. Parmesan, finely grated (about 1 cup), plus more for serving

RECIPE PREPARATION

1. Cook pasta in a large pot of boiling salted water, stirring occasionally and adding peas about 2 minutes before pasta is done, until al dente. Drain pasta and peas, reserving 1½ cups pasta cooking liquid.

2. Meanwhile, heat butter in a large Dutch oven or other heavy pot over medium until frothy. Tear prosciutto slices into bite-size pieces and add to pot along with sage. Cook, stirring occasionally, until prosciutto is golden brown and beginning to crisp, about 4 minutes. Remove from heat and let sit until pasta is done.

3. Add pasta, peas, 2 oz. Parmesan, and 1 cup reserved pasta cooking liquid to pot with

prosciutto and return to medium heat. Cook, tossing vigorously and adding more pasta cooking liquid if needed, until saucy and pasta is coated, about 30 seconds. Taste and season with more salt if needed.
4. Divide pasta among bowls and top with more Parmesan.

Red Pesto Pasta
INGREDIENTS
- 6 oil-packed anchovy fillets
- 4 garlic cloves, smashed
- ¾ cup extra-virgin olive oil
- ½ cup walnuts
- 3 Tbsp. double-concentrated tomato paste
- 2 red Fresno chiles, split lengthwise, seeds removed
- 3 Tbsp. fresh lemon juice
- 3 oz. finely grated Parmesan, plus more for serving
- ½ tsp. kosher salt, plus more
- 1 lb. spaghetti

- 2 Tbsp. unsalted butter, cut into pieces

RECIPE PREPARATION

1. Cook anchovies, garlic, oil, and walnuts in a small saucepan over medium heat, stirring often, until walnuts are deeply golden and garlic is just beginning to turn golden, 4–5 minutes. Add tomato paste and cook, stirring often, until it turns a shade darker, about 2 minutes. Remove pan from heat and let cool 5 minutes.

2. Transfer walnut mixture (including the oil) to a food processor. Add chiles, lemon juice, 3 oz. Parmesan, and ½ tsp. salt. Pulse until a thick paste forms.

3. Meanwhile, cook pasta in a large pot of boiling salted water, stirring occasionally, until al dente. Drain pasta, reserving 1½ cups pasta cooking liquid.

4. Scrape pesto into a large bowl and add butter, then pasta and ½ cup pasta cooking liquid. Using tongs, toss pasta vigorously, adding more pasta cooking liquid if needed (you may

not need all of it), until glossy and well coated with sauce.

5. Divide pasta among bowls. Season with more salt and top with Parmesan.
6. Do Ahead: Pesto can be made 5 days ahead. Cover and chill.

Creamy Pasta with Crispy Mushrooms
INGREDIENTS
- 4 Tbsp. extra-virgin olive oil
- 1 lb. mixed mushrooms (such as maitake, oyster, crimini, and/or shiitake), torn into bite-size pieces
- Kosher salt
- 2 medium shallots, finely chopped
- 1 lb. spaghetti or bucatini
- ½ cup heavy cream
- ⅓ cup finely chopped parsley
- Zest and juice of ½ lemon
- 2 Tbsp. unsalted butter, cut into pieces
- ½ oz. Parmesan, finely grated (about ½ cup), plus more for serving

- Freshly ground black pepper

RECIPE PREPARATION

1. Heat 2 Tbsp. oil in a large pot over medium-high. Cook half of mushrooms in a single layer, undisturbed, until edges are brown and starting to crisp, about 3 minutes. Give mushrooms a toss and continue to cook, tossing occasionally, until all sides are brown and crisp, about 5 minutes more. Using a slotted spoon, transfer mushrooms to a plate; season with salt. Repeat with remaining 2 Tbsp. oil and mushrooms and more salt.
2. Reduce heat to medium-low and return all of the mushrooms to the pot. Add shallots and cook, stirring often, until shallots are translucent and softened, about 2 minutes.
3. Meanwhile, cook pasta in a large pot of boiling salted water, stirring occasionally, until very al dente, about 2 minutes less than package directions.
4. Using tongs, transfer pasta to pot with mushrooms and add cream and 1 cup pasta

cooking liquid. Increase heat to medium, bring to a simmer, and cook, tossing constantly, until pasta is al dente and liquid is slightly thickened, about 3 minutes.

5. Remove pot from heat. Add lemon zest and juice, parsley, butter, ½ oz. Parmesan, and lots of pepper and toss to combine. Taste and season with more salt if needed.

6. Divide pasta among bowls and top with more Parmesan.

Spaghetti with No-Cook Puttanesca
INGREDIENTS
- 2 beefsteak tomatoes (about 1 lb.), halved crosswise, seeds removed
- 2 garlic cloves, finely grated
- 1 tsp. crushed red pepper flakes
- 2 tsp. kosher salt, plus more
- 1½ cups cherry tomatoes, halved
- 1 cup Castelvetrano olives, crushed, pits removed
- 2 Tbsp. drained capers

- ¼ cup extra-virgin olive oil, plus more for drizzling
- 12 oz. spaghetti
- ¼ cup finely chopped parsley
- 3 Tbsp. unsalted butter, cut into pieces

RECIPE PREPARATION

1. Pulse beefsteak tomatoes, garlic, red pepper flakes, and 2 tsp. salt in a food processor until smooth; transfer sauce to a large bowl and mix in cherry tomatoes, olives, capers, and ¼ cup oil.
2. Cook spaghetti in a large pot of boiling salted water, stirring occasionally, until al dente. Drain pasta, reserving ¼ cup pasta cooking liquid.
3. Add pasta, parsley, and butter to sauce. Toss vigorously with tongs, adding a splash of pasta cooking liquid or more as needed to create an emulsified sauce that coats pasta. Divide among bowls and drizzle with more oil.

Pasta With Brown Butter, Whole Lemon, and Parmesan

INGREDIENTS

- 1 lb. short tube pasta (such as paccheri or rigatoni)
- Kosher salt
- 8 Tbsp. (1 stick) unsalted butter, cut into pieces, divided
- 1 small regular lemon or Meyer lemon, very thinly sliced into rounds, seeds removed
- 1 oz. Parmesan, finely grated, plus more for serving
- Freshly ground black pepper

RECIPE PREPARATION

1. Cook pasta in a large pot of boiling generously salted water, stirring occasionally, until very al dente, about 2 minutes less than package directions (pasta will finish cooking in the sauce).
2. Meanwhile, heat half of the butter in a large Dutch oven or other heavy pot over medium until melted. Add lemon slices and cook,

stirring often, until softened and bottom of pot is browned in spots, 5–7 minutes. Using tongs, transfer one-third of lemon slices to a plate; set aside.

3. Just before pasta is al dente, scoop out 2 cups pasta cooking liquid. Add 1½ cups pasta cooking liquid to butter sauce. (This may seem like a lot of liquid, but it will thicken once the remaining ingredients are added.) Add remaining butter a piece at a time, whisking until each piece is incorporated before adding more, until the sauce is emulsified and creamy.

4. Drain pasta and add to sauce. Cook, stirring often and adding 1 oz. Parmesan a little at a time. Once all of the cheese is added, continue to cook, still stirring, until cheese is melted and sauce is creamy and clings to pasta, about 3 minutes. If sauce looks very thick, add more pasta cooking liquid 1–2 Tbsp. at a time to thin (saucier is ideal as it will thicken as it cools). Remove from heat

and sprinkle with an almost ridiculous amount of pepper (about 2 tsp.); toss once more.
5. Serve pasta topped with reserved lemon rounds and more Parmesan.

Fusilli With Battuto di Erbe
INGREDIENTS
- 1¼ cups extra-virgin olive oil, divided
- 1 garlic clove, smashed
- 1 oz. mixed hardy herb leaves (such as rosemary, sage, thyme, and/or marjoram; about 1 heaping cup)
- 1 tsp. fennel pollen (optional)
- 7 oz. tender spring greens (such as arugula, dandelion, and/or broccoli rabe leaves; about 5 cups)
- 5 oz. mixed tender herb leaves (suchas mint, basil, lovage, celery leaves, and/or parsley; about 6 cups)
- ½ tsp. kosher salt, plus more
- 1 lb. fusilli (spiral-shaped pasta)

RECIPE PREPARATION

Do ahead:

- Heat ¾ cup oil in a large Dutch oven or other heavy pot over medium until shimmering. Add garlic, hardy herbs, fennel pollen (if using), and red pepper flakes and cook, stirring often, until oil around garlic starts to sizzle slightly and garlic begins to turn golden brown, about 2 minutes (be careful when you add the garlic as the oil may spatter). Add spring greens and tender herbs and season with a couple pinches of salt. Cook, stirring often, until greens and herbs are wilted and bright green, about 2 minutes. Scrape herb mixture onto a rimmed baking sheet; spread out and let cool slightly. Reserve pot.
- Transfer herb mixture to a blender or food processor and add ½ tsp. salt and remaining ½ cup oil; blend on high speed until you have a coarse purée. Taste pesto and season with more salt if needed.

- Cook pasta in a large pot of boiling salted water, stirring occasionally, until al dente. Drain pasta, reserving 1 cup pasta cooking liquid.
- Scrape pesto back into reserved pot and add pasta and ¾ cup pasta cooking liquid. Set over medium-low heat and cook, tossing vigorously and adding more pasta cooking liquid if needed, until warmed through and pasta is coated (do not let pesto come to a boil), about 1 minute. Taste and season with more salt if needed.
- Divide pasta among bowls. Using a mandoline or vegetable peeler, shave cheese over pasta.
- Pesto can be made 1 day ahead. Transfer to a bowl set in a larger bowl of ice water and let cool. Remove bowl with pesto from water; cover tightly and chill.

Red Wine Spaghetti
INGREDIENTS

- 12 garlic cloves, finely chopped
- 3 Tbsp. extra-virgin olive oil, plus more for drizzling
- 1 tsp. crushed red pepper flakes
- 16 Tbsp. (2 sticks) unsalted butter, cut into 1" pieces, divided
- 2 750-ml bottles red wine
- Kosher salt
- 2 lb. spaghetti
- Finely grated Parmesan (for serving)

RECIPE PREPARATION

1. Combine garlic and 3 Tbsp. oil in a small bowl. Heat a large Dutch oven or other heavy pot over medium; pour in garlic and oil. Add red pepper flakes and 2 Tbsp. butter; cook, stirring occasionally, until garlic is very fragrant but not browned, about 3 minutes. Add wine, increase heat to medium-high, and bring to a boil. Cook, uncovered, until reduced by two-thirds, 20–25 minutes; season with salt. Cover and keep warm.

2. Meanwhile, cook pasta in a pot of salted boiling water, stirring occasionally, until very al dente, about 3 minutes shy of recommended cook time.
3. Drain pasta and add to sauce, along with remaining 14 Tbsp. butter. Set pot over medium heat and bring sauce to a simmer. Cook, tossing often, until pasta is well coated and sauce is thickened, about 3 minutes. Taste and season with more salt if needed.
4. Divide pasta among bowls; drizzle with oil and top with lots of Parmesan.

Brothy Pasta with Chickpeas
INGREDIENTS
- 3 Tbsp. extra-virgin olive oil, plus more for drizzling
- 1 small onion, finely chopped
- Kosher salt
- 3 garlic cloves, thinly sliced
- 1 sprig rosemary
- ¼ tsp. crushed red pepper flakes

- 1 15-oz. can chickpeas, drained, rinsed
- 1 cup whole peeled tomatoes, crushed by hand
- 6 oz. orecchiette or other short pasta
- 2 Tbsp. finely chopped parsley
- 3 Tbsp. finely grated Parmesan, plus more for serving
- Freshly ground black pepper

RECIPE PREPARATION

1. Heat 3 Tbsp. oil in a large saucepan over medium. Add onion and season with salt. Cook, stirring occasionally, until onion is beginning to soften, about 5 minutes. Add garlic and continue to cook, stirring occasionally, until onion and garlic are both very soft and just beginning to brown around the edges, 5–6 minutes longer. Add rosemary and red pepper flakes and cook, stirring, until fragrant, about 30 seconds. Add chickpeas and tomatoes and cook, stirring occasionally, until tomatoes are slightly thickened, 6–8 minutes.

2. Add pasta and 4 cups water. Increase heat to medium-high, bring to a simmer, and cook, stirring occasionally to prevent pasta from sticking, until pasta is al dente, 13–16 minutes depending on shape. Stir in parsley and 3 Tbsp. Parmesan; season with salt.
3. Divide brothy pasta between bowls. Drizzle with more oil and top with Parmesan and black pepper.

Bucatini Alla Griccia With Fava Beans
INGREDIENTS
- 1 Tbsp. black peppercorns
- 8 oz. guanciale (salt-cured pork jowl)
- 1¾ cups fresh fava beans (from about 1¾ lb. pods) or frozen fava beans
- 1 lb. bucatini
- 2 oz. Pecorino Romano, finely grated (about 1 cup), plus more for serving

RECIPE PREPARATION
1. Place peppercorns in a bag, close, and coarsely crush with a rolling pin or heavy

skillet (alternatively, you can crush them directly on a cutting board set inside a large rimmed baking sheet). Slice guanciale into ¼"-thick slabs, then slice slabs crosswise into ¼"-thick matchsticks.

2. If using fresh fava beans, cook in a large pot of boiling salted water until just tender (the best way to gauge doneness is to check one; be sure to slip it from its skin before tasting!), about 3 minutes. Using a spider or slotted spoon, transfer to a bowl of ice water; let cool. Drain and peel away outer skin from each bean; discard skins. Reserve pot with boiling water for cooking pasta.

3. Place guanciale in a dry large Dutch oven or other heavy pot and set over medium-high heat. Cook, stirring often with a wooden spoon, until golden brown and crisp, about 5 minutes. Add crushed peppercorns and stir once to combine. Add 1 cup hot tap water (using pasta cooking liquid here could make the dish too salty) and bring to a boil. Remove

pot from heat and stir mixture aggressively to emulsify. Let sit until pasta is done.
4. Return reserved pot of water to a boil and cook pasta, stirring occasionally (if using frozen fava beans, add about 2 minutes before pasta is done), until al dente. Drain pasta and fava beans.

Burst Cherry Tomato Pasta
INGREDIENTS
- ½ cup extra-virgin olive oil, plus more for drizzling
- 6 garlic cloves, smashed
- 4 pints cherry tomatoes (about 2½ lb.)
- ¾ tsp. crushed red pepper flakes
- 2 large sprigs basil, plus 1 cup basil leaves, torn if large
- 1½ tsp. kosher salt, plus more
- Pinch of sugar (optional)
- 12 oz. campanelle or other tube pasta
- 1 oz. finely grated Parmesan (about ⅓ cup), plus more for serving

RECIPE PREPARATION

1. Heat ½ cup oil in a large heavy pot over low. Add garlic and cook, stirring, until softened and fragrant but not browned, about 2 minutes. Increase heat to medium and add tomatoes, red pepper flakes, basil sprigs, and 1½ tsp. salt. Cook, stirring to coat, until tomatoes begin to burst, about 4 minutes. Smash some but not all of the tomatoes with the back of a wooden spoon to help create a sauce, then continue to cook, stirring occasionally, until a chunky, thickened sauce comes together and about half the tomatoes are completely broken down and half remain in tact, 10–12 minutes. Taste and adjust seasoning, adding sugar if sauce seems tart. Pluck out and discard basil sprigs.

2. Meanwhile, cook pasta in a large pot of boiling salted water, stirring occasionally, until al dente. Drain pasta, add to pot with sauce, and cook over medium heat, stirring,

until coated, 1–2 minutes. Remove from heat and stir in 1 oz. Parmesan.
3. Divide pasta among bowls. Top with more Parmesan and 1 cup basil leaves. Drizzle with oil.

Pasta with Sausage and Arugula
INGREDIENTS
- 2 small red onions, sliced into ½"-thick wedges
- 1 fennel bulb, sliced into ½"-thick wedges
- 6 Tbsp. extra-virgin olive oil, divided
- Kosher salt, freshly ground pepper
- 8 oz. hot or sweet Italian sausage (about 2 links), casings removed
- 10 oz. gemelli, casarecce, or other medium pasta
- 1 tsp. finely grated lemon zest
- 2 Tbsp. fresh lemon juice
- 6 cups baby arugula
- Finely grated Parmesan (for serving)

RECIPE PREPARATION

1. Preheat oven to 425°. Toss onions, fennel, and 2 Tbsp. oil on a rimmed baking sheet; season with salt and pepper. Spread out into a single layer. Pinch sausage into small pieces and scatter around onions and fennel. Roast until vegetables and sausage are cooked through and well browned, 25–30 minutes.
2. Meanwhile, cook pasta in a large pot of boiling salted water, stirring occasionally, until al dente. Drain, reserving 1 cup pasta cooking liquid.
3. Combine vegetables, sausage, and pasta in a large bowl. Add lemon zest, lemon juice, remaining 4 Tbsp. oil, and ¼ cup reserved pasta cooking liquid and toss to coat, adding more pasta cooking liquid if needed, until sauce comes together and coats pasta. Toss in arugula.
4. Divide pasta among plates and top with Parmesan. Season with more salt and pepper.

Rigatoni With Fennel and Anchovies

INGREDIENTS

- 3 large fennel bulbs (about 2½ lb.)
- ½ cup extra-virgin olive oil
- 6 oil-packed anchovy fillets
- 6 garlic cloves, thinly sliced
- ½ tsp. crushed red pepper flakes
- ½ cup (packed) mint leaves, plus more torn for serving
- 1 orange or tangerine
- 1 lemon
- 1 lb. rigatoni
- 3 oz. Pecorino Romano, finely grated (about 1½ cups)

RECIPE PREPARATION

1. Remove tough outer layers and fronds from fennel bulbs and discard. Working one at a time, cut bulbs lengthwise (through root ends) into quarters, remove cores, and slice quarters lengthwise into ½"-thick wedges.

2. Heat oil in a large Dutch oven or other heavy pot over high until shimmering. Add fennel

to pot, arranging in as even a layer as possible. Season with salt and cook, undisturbed, until golden brown underneath and starting to soften, 6–8 minutes. Using tongs, turn fennel over and cook until golden brown on the other side, 6–8 minutes.

3. Reduce heat to low and add anchovies, garlic, red pepper flakes, and ½ cup mint to pot. Cook, stirring often, until anchovies are disintegrated and garlic is golden, about 2 minutes. Remove pot from heat and finely grate zest of orange and lemon directly into hot oil; stir well to evenly distribute. Cover pot to keep sauce warm and let sit until pasta is done.

4. Meanwhile, cook pasta in a large pot of boiling salted water, stirring occasionally, until al dente. Drain pasta, reserving 1½ cups pasta cooking liquid.

5. Uncover sauce, add pasta and 1 cup reserved pasta cooking liquid, and set over medium-low heat. Add Pecorino and cook, tossing

vigorously and adding more pasta cooking liquid if needed, until sauce is emulsified and pasta is coated, about 2 minutes.
6. Divide pasta among bowls and top with torn mint.

Broccoli Bolognese with Orecchiette
INGREDIENTS
- 1 large head of broccoli (1¼–1½ pounds), cut into florets, stalk peeled and chopped into ½" pieces
- Kosher salt
- 2 tablespoons extra-virgin olive oil, plus more for drizzling
- 4 garlic cloves, smashed
- 12 ounces fresh Italian sausage (about 3 links), casings removed
- Crushed red pepper flakes
- 12 ounces orecchiette
- 3 tablespoons unsalted butter, cut into pieces
- 1½ ounces Parmesan, finely grated (about ½ cup), plus more for serving

RECIPE PREPARATION
1. Cook broccoli in a large pot of salted boiling water until crisp-tender, about 3 minutes. Using a slotted spoon, transfer broccoli to a colander and let cool (save pot of water for cooking pasta). Chop broccoli into small pieces; set aside.
2. Heat 2 Tbsp. oil in a large skillet over medium. Cook garlic, shaking skillet occasionally, until it starts to turn golden, about 2 minutes. Transfer garlic to a small bowl. Cook sausage and a generous pinch of red pepper flakes, breaking up meat into smaller pieces with a wooden spoon and stirring occasionally, until browned and cooked through, 6–8 minutes.
3. Bring reserved pot of water to a boil and cook pasta until barely al dente, about 9 minutes (set a timer for 3 minutes less than the package instructions; it will cook more in the skillet).

4. Meanwhile, ladle about ½ cup pasta cooking liquid from pot into skillet with sausage and add garlic and blanched broccoli. Keep mixture at a low simmer, stirring often and mashing with a potato masher to break up sausage even more, until pasta is finished cooking.
5. Using a spider or slotted spoon, transfer pasta to skillet, then ladle in ½ cup pasta water. Cook, stirring, until pasta absorbs most of the liquid and is just al dente, about 4 minutes. Add butter and stir until melted, then transfer pasta to a large bowl. Gradually add 1½ oz. Parmesan, tossing constantly until you have a glossy, emulsified sauce.
6. Serve pasta topped with more Parmesan and red pepper flakes and a drizzle of oil.

Rigatoni With Fennel and Anchovies
INGREDIENTS
- 3 large fennel bulbs (about 2½ lb.)
- ½ cup extra-virgin olive oil

- 6 oil-packed anchovy fillets
- 6 garlic cloves, thinly sliced
- ½ tsp. crushed red pepper flakes
- ½ cup (packed) mint leaves, plus more torn for serving
- 1 orange or tangerine
- 1 lemon
- 1 lb. rigatoni
- 3 oz. Pecorino Romano, finely grated (about 1½ cups)

RECIPE PREPARATION

1. Remove tough outer layers and fronds from fennel bulbs and discard. Working one at a time, cut bulbs lengthwise (through root ends) into quarters, remove cores, and slice quarters lengthwise into ½"-thick wedges.
2. Heat oil in a large Dutch oven or other heavy pot over high until shimmering. Add fennel to pot, arranging in as even a layer as possible. Season with salt and cook, undisturbed, until golden brown underneath and starting to soften, 6–8 minutes. Using

tongs, turn fennel over and cook until golden brown on the other side, 6–8 minutes.

3. Reduce heat to low and add anchovies, garlic, red pepper flakes, and ½ cup mint to pot. Cook, stirring often, until anchovies are disintegrated and garlic is golden, about 2 minutes. Remove pot from heat and finely grate zest of orange and lemon directly into hot oil; stir well to evenly distribute. Cover pot to keep sauce warm and let sit until pasta is done.

4. Meanwhile, cook pasta in a large pot of boiling salted water, stirring occasionally, until al dente. Drain pasta, reserving 1½ cups pasta cooking liquid.

5. Uncover sauce, add pasta and 1 cup reserved pasta cooking liquid, and set over medium-low heat. Add Pecorino and cook, tossing vigorously and adding more pasta cooking liquid if needed, until sauce is emulsified and pasta is coated, about 2 minutes.

6. Divide pasta among bowls and top with torn mint.

Kale Pesto With Whole Wheat Pasta
INGREDIENTS
- 1 large bunch Tuscan kale, ribs and stems removed
- Kosher salt
- 12 oz. farro pasta or whole wheat pasta
- ⅓ cup raw pistachios
- ¼ cup extra-virgin olive oil
- 1 garlic clove
- 1 oz. Parmesan, finely grated, plus more for serving
- 2 Tbsp. unsalted butter
- Freshly ground black pepper

RECIPE PREPARATION
1. Cook kale leaves in a large pot of boiling salted water until bright green and wilted, about 30 seconds. Transfer to a rimmed baking sheet with tongs; keep water boiling.

Let kale cool slightly; wring out excess water with your hands.
2. Cook pasta in pot of boiling water, stirring occasionally, until al dente.
3. Blend nuts, oil, garlic, and ⅓ cup water in a blender or food processor until very smooth. Add kale and 1 oz. Parmesan. Purée, adding water 1 Tbsp. at a time as needed, until smooth. Transfer pesto to a large bowl.
4. Using tongs, transfer pasta to bowl with pesto; add butter and ⅓ cup pasta cooking liquid. Toss, adding more pasta cooking liquid by the tablespoonful if needed, until sauce coats pasta. Divide among bowls; top with more Parmesan and a few grinds of pepper.

Tuna Niçoise Salad
INGREDIENTS
- ¾ cup extra-virgin olive oil
- ¼ cup fresh lemon juice
- 2 Tbsp. Dijon mustard

- 1 tsp. honey
- 1 tsp. freshly ground black pepper
- 1 tsp. kosher salt, plus more
- 6 large eggs
- 1 lb. green beans, trimmed and/or new or baby potatoes, halved if larger
- 4 cups seedless cucumbers
- 3 cups oil-packed tuna
- Olives, capers, peperoncini, pickles, or other pickled-briny ingredients (for serving)
- Flaky sea salt

RECIPE PREPARATION

1. Whisk oil, lemon juice, mustard, honey, pepper, and 1 tsp. kosher salt in a medium bowl; set dressing aside.
2. Bring a medium pot of salted water to a boil. Carefully add eggs and cook 7 minutes. Using a slotted spoon, transfer eggs to a bowl of ice water (keep pot over high heat); chill until cold, about 5 minutes. Peel; set aside.
3. Meanwhile, add green beans and potatoes to the same pot of boiling water and cook until

just tender, 2–4 minutes for green beans, 10–15 minutes for potatoes. Using a slotted spoon, transfer to bowl of ice water; let sit until cold, about 3 minutes. Transfer to paper towels; pat dry.

4. To serve, slice eggs in half and arrange on a platter with cooked and raw vegetables and tuna. Top with pickled-briny ingredient(s), sprinkle with sea salt, and drizzle some reserved dressing over. Serve with remaining dressing alongside.

5. Do Ahead: Dressing can be made 5 days ahead; cover and chill. Eggs can be boiled and vegetables blanched 2 days ahead; cover and chill separately.

Roasted Squash and Cauliflower With Cashew Tonnato

INGREDIENTS

- 1 delicata squash (about 1½ pounds), halved lengthwise, seeds removed, sliced crosswise into ¾-inch pieces
- 1 medium head of cauliflower (about 2½ pounds), trimmed, core removed, cut into 1-inch pieces
- ½ cup plus 2 tablespoons extra-virgin olive oil, divided, plus more for drizzling
- Kosher salt, freshly ground pepper
- 3 oil-packed anchovy fillets
- ½ Fresno chile, seeds removed, coarsely chopped
- 1 large garlic clove
- 1 6.7-ounce jar of tuna in olive oil, drained, larger pieces broken up
- ¾ cup raw cashews, divided
- 4 tablespoons fresh lemon juice, divided, plus more
- 1 tablespoon black sesame seeds

- 1 tablespoon coriander seeds
- 1 teaspoon fennel seeds
- 1 teaspoon crushed red pepper flakes
- 4 cups (loosely packed) mature arugula, torn
- 1 tablespoon drained capers
- Lemon wedges (for serving)

Special Equipment
- A spice mill or mortar and pestle

RECIPE PREPARATION

1. Arrange racks in upper and lower thirds of oven; preheat to 400°. Place squash on one rimmed baking sheet and cauliflower on another one. Drizzle squash with 1 Tbsp. oil, season with salt and pepper, and toss to coat. Drizzle cauliflower with 2 Tbsp. oil, season with salt and pepper, and toss to coat. Roast squash and cauliflower, tossing and rotating sheets halfway through, until squash is browned and tender, 35–40 minutes, and cauliflower is browned and tender with charred edges, 40–45 minutes.

2. Meanwhile, combine anchovies, chile, garlic, tuna, ½ cup cashews, 2 Tbsp. lemon juice, 6 Tbsp. oil, and 3 Tbsp. hot water in a blender and let soak 5 minutes. Purée on low speed, gradually increasing to high, until sauce is very smooth. Season tonnato with salt and pepper.
3. Toast sesame seeds, coriander seeds, and fennel seeds in a small skillet over medium heat, stirring, until fragrant, about 2 minutes. Transfer to a small bowl and let cool. Heat 1 Tbsp. oil in same skillet. Toast remaining ¼ cup cashews, tossing, until golden brown, about 3 minutes. Using a slotted spoon, transfer cashews to a plate. Pour off cashew oil into a small bowl.
4. Transfer toasted spices to spice mill or mortar and pestle and coarsely grind, then add to bowl with cashew oil. Coarsely grind cashews in spice mill or with mortar and pestle (with pieces no larger than ¼"). Transfer to bowl with spices. Add red pepper

flakes and stir to combine (the dukkah should look like coarse wet sand).
5. Gently toss squash, cauliflower, and arugula in a large bowl.
6. Swipe ¼ cup tonnato on a plate. Top with one-quarter of squash mixture, then sprinkle with dukkah and capers. Drizzle with oil. Serve with lemon wedges alongside.

Green Goddess Tuna Salad Sandwich
INGREDIENTS
- ¼ cup basil leaves
- ¼ cup parsley leaves with tender stems
- ¼ cup tarragon leaves
- ¼ cup mayonnaise
- ¼ cup sour cream
- 1 tsp. finely grated lemon zest
- 2 Tbsp. plus 1 tsp. fresh lemon juice
- 2 Tbsp. extra-virgin olive oil, plus more for drizzling
- 1 5-oz. can tuna in water, drained
- 1 celery stalk, finely chopped

- 1 small shallot, finely chopped
- 1 garlic clove, finely grated
- Kosher salt, freshly ground pepper
- ½ cup coarsely chopped mixed tender herbs (such as celery leaves, basil, parsley, and/or dill)
- 2 English muffins, split, lightly toasted

RECIPE PREPARATION

1. Purée basil, parsley, tarragon, mayonnaise, sour cream, lemon zest, 2 Tbsp. lemon juice, and 2 Tbsp. oil in a blender until very smooth and pale green. Transfer dressing to a medium bowl and add tuna. Using a fork, break up tuna and incorporate into dressing. Mix in celery, shallot, and garlic; season with salt and lots of pepper.
2. Toss chopped mixed herbs with remaining 1 tsp. lemon juice in a small bowl. Drizzle with a little oil, season with salt and pepper, and toss again.

3. Build sandwiches with English muffins, tuna salad (you may have a bit extra), and herb salad.

Escarole Caesar With Sardines and Hazelnuts
INGREDIENTS
- ½ cup blanched hazelnuts
- 1 3.75-oz. can sardines, drained
- 1 garlic clove, finely grated
- 2 Tbsp. fresh lemon juice
- 1 tsp. Dijon mustard
- ½ tsp. freshly ground black pepper, plus more
- 1½ oz. Piave cheese or Parmesan, divided
- ½ cup mayonnaise
- 2 Tbsp. extra-virgin olive oil
- Kosher salt
- 1 large head or 2 small heads of escarole (about 1½ lb.), wilted outer leaves removed, inner leaves torn into large pieces
- Lemon wedges (for serving)

RECIPE PREPARATION
1. Preheat oven to 325°. Toast hazelnuts on a rimmed baking sheet until deep golden brown, 12–15 minutes. Let cool, then crush or coarsely chop.
2. Open each sardine with the tip of a paring knife, prying the fillets apart. Remove any bones. Finely chop 2 sardines and transfer to a large bowl. Add garlic, lemon juice, mustard, and ½ tsp. pepper and whisk to combine. Finely grate 1 oz. Piave (about two-thirds) into bowl and add mayonnaise and oil; whisk to combine. Season dressing with salt.
3. Add escarole and three-fourths of hazelnuts to bowl with dressing and toss well to coat; season with salt and pepper.
4. Divide salad among plates, top with remaining hazelnuts. Shave remaining ½ oz. Piave over and break remaining sardines into smaller pieces and scatter on top. Serve with lemon wedges for squeezing over.

Charred Green Beans with Spicy Tonnato

INGREDIENTS

- 1 habanero chile, seeds removed, quartered
- 2 oil-packed anchovy fillets
- 1 6.7-ounce jar oil-packed tuna, drained
- ½ cup mayonnaise
- 3 tablespoons fresh lime juice
- 1 tablespoon drained capers
- ¼ cup plus 2 tablespoons olive oil
- Kosher salt
- 2 pounds mixed snap beans, such as green, wax, and/or Romano, cleaned, trimmed
- Cilantro leaves with tender stems, salted, roasted pumpkin seeds (pepitas), and lime wedges (for serving)

RECIPE PREPARATION

1. Purée chile, anchovies, tuna, mayonnaise, lime juice, capers, ¼ cup oil, and 2 Tbsp. water in a blender until smooth. Season tonnato with salt.
2. Prepare a grill for medium-high heat. Toss beans in a medium bowl with remaining 2 Tbsp. oil; season with salt. Working in

batches if needed, grill beans in a single layer (if you have a perforated grill pan, this is the perfect time to use it!), turning frequently, until charred on all sides, about 6 minutes.
3. Pour one-quarter of tonnato on a platter. Arrange beans over, then drizzle with remaining tonnato. Top with some cilantro and pumpkin seeds and squeeze a little lime juice over.

Toast with Tomato Jam, Boquerones, and Lemon Oil
INGREDIENTS
- 2 pounds vine-ripened or plum tomatoes
- ½ cup olive oil, divided, plus more for drizzling
- Kosher salt
- 1 lemon, zest removed in wide strips, thinly sliced lengthwise
- 6 ½-inch-thick baguette slices cut on a diagonal, toasted
- 6 boquerones (marinated white anchovies)

- 6 oil-packed anchovies
- 3 scallions, dark-green parts only, thinly sliced on a steep diagonal

RECIPE PREPARATION

1. Preheat oven to 300°. Using a paring knife, score a shallow X on the bottom of each tomato. Working in batches, cook tomatoes in a large ovenproof pot of boiling water just until skins at X begin to peel back, 15–30 seconds. Using a slotted spoon, transfer tomatoes to a bowl of ice water and let cool. Peel tomatoes. Remove cores, then halve lengthwise and scrape out seeds. Transfer tomatoes back to pot, crushing with your hands. Mix in ¼ cup oil, cover, and bake until tomatoes are slightly darkened and very soft, 2–3 hours.

2. Transfer pot to stovetop, uncover, and cook over medium-low, stirring occasionally, until deep red and thickened, 45–70 minutes; season with salt. Transfer to an airtight container and let cool.

3. While tomatoes are baking, heat lemon zest and ¼ cup oil in a small saucepan over low 5 minutes. Let cool.
4. Spoon about 1 Tbsp. tomato jam over top of each toast. Top each with a boquerone and anchovy fillet; drizzle with lemon oil and scatter scallion tops over.
5. Do Ahead: Tomato jam can be made 5 days ahead; cover and chill. Lemon oil can be made 2 weeks ahead; store airtight at room temperature.

Trout Toast with Soft Scrambled Eggs
INGREDIENTS
- 8 large eggs
- ¾ tsp. kosher salt, plus more
- 6 Tbsp. unsalted butter, divided
- 4 1"-thick slices sourdough or country-style bread
- 3 Tbsp. crème fraîche or sour cream

- 1 skin-on, boneless smoked trout fillet (about 5 oz.), skin removed, flesh broken into 1" pieces
- 1 lemon, halved
- Freshly ground black pepper
- 2 scallions, thinly sliced on a diagonal
- 2 Tbsp. coarsely chopped dill
- 4 oz. mature arugula, tough stems trimmed (about 4 cups)
- 2 tsp. extra-virgin olive oil

RECIPE PREPARATION

1. Crack eggs into a medium bowl and add ¾ tsp. salt. Whisk until no streaks remain.
2. Heat 2 Tbsp. butter in a large nonstick skillet over medium. As soon as foaming subsides, add 2 slices of bread and cook until golden brown underneath, about 3 minutes. Transfer to plates, cooked side up. Repeat with another 2 Tbsp. butter and remaining 2 slices of bread. Season toast with salt. Wipe out skillet and let it cool 3 minutes.

3. Heat remaining 2 Tbsp. butter in reserved skillet over medium-low. Once butter is foaming, cook egg mixture, stirring with a heatproof rubber spatula in broad sweeping motions, until some curds begin to form but eggs are still runny, about 2 minutes. Stir in crème fraîche and cook, stirring occasionally, until eggs are barely set, about 1 minute.
4. Spoon eggs over toast and top with trout. Finely grate lemon zest from one of the lemon halves over trout, then squeeze juice over toast. Season with pepper; scatter scallions and dill on top.
5. Squeeze juice from remaining lemon half into a medium bowl. Add arugula and drizzle with oil; season with salt and pepper. Toss to coat. Mound alongside toasts.

Tuna Casserole with Dill and Potato Chips
INGREDIENTS
- ½ cup (1 stick) plus 1 tablespoon unsalted butter, divided
- 12 ounces dried curly egg noodles
- Kosher salt
- 1 large onion, finely chopped
- 1 medium leek, white and pale-green parts only, finely chopped
- 10 ounces mushrooms (such as crimini, shiitake, and/or button mushrooms), chopped
- ¼ cup white wine
- Freshly ground black pepper
- 1 tablespoon Worcestershire sauce
- 2 teaspoons finely chopped thyme
- ¼ cup all-purpose flour
- 2½ cups homemade chicken stock or low-sodium chicken broth
- 1 cup heavy cream
- 6 ounces white cheddar, grated
- 2 teaspoons hot sauce (preferably Tabasco)

- 2 6-ounce jars oil-packed tuna, drained, broken into small pieces
- 2 cups potato chips
- 1 lemon
- ½ cup dill, coarsely chopped
- 2 tablespoons finely chopped chives

RECIPE PREPARATION

1. Preheat oven to 400°. Grease a 13x9" baking dish with 1 Tbsp. butter.
2. Cook egg noodles in a large pot of boiling salted water, stirring occasionally, until very al dente, about 2 minutes. Drain pasta; let cool.
3. Melt 4 Tbsp. butter in a large skillet over medium heat. Add onion and leek; cook, stirring, until soft but not brown, 8–10 minutes. Increase heat to medium-high and add mushrooms. Cook, tossing occasionally, until most of the mushroom liquid has evaporated, 4–6 minutes. Add wine and reduce until skillet is almost dry, about 2

minutes; season with salt and pepper. Stir in Worcestershire and thyme.

4. Melt remaining 4 Tbsp. butter in a medium pot over medium-low heat. Whisk in flour and cook until roux is golden and looks shiny and smooth, about 2 minutes. Whisking constantly, add chicken stock and bring to a boil. Reduce heat to medium and add cream, cheddar, and hot sauce; cook, stirring, until cheese is melted, about 1 minute. Season with salt and pepper.

5. Gently fold mushroom mixture, cream mixture, noodles, and tuna in a large bowl; taste and adjust seasonings if needed.

6. Transfer tuna mixture to prepared baking dish. Press chips into casserole so they stand upright. Bake casserole until bubbly around the edges and chips begin to brown, 15–20 minutes. Zest one-quarter of the lemon over casserole. Let sit 5 minutes, then top with dill and chives.

Pan Bagnat

INGREDIENTS
- 2 oil-packed anchovy fillets, drained, finely chopped
- 2 small garlic cloves, finely grated
- 2 tablespoons capers, drained, chopped
- 2 tablespoons red wine vinegar
- 1 tablespoon Dijon mustard
- 1 small red onion, very thinly sliced
- 1 cup mixed olives (such as niçoise, kalamata, and/or Castelvetrano), coarsely chopped
- 4 tablespoons extra-virgin olive oil, divided, plus more for drizzling
- Kosher salt, freshly ground pepper
- 1 6–7-ounce jar oil-packed tuna, drained
- ½ lemon
- ½ baguette, lightly toasted
- 1½ cups basil leaves, torn
- 1½ cups parsley leaves with tender stems, coarsely chopped
- 2 large hard-boiled eggs, peeled, thinly sliced
- 1 large tomato, sliced

- 2 jarred roasted red peppers, sliced

RECIPE PREPARATION

1. Mix anchovies, garlic, capers, vinegar, and mustard in a medium bowl. Add onion and olives and let sit, tossing occasionally, until onion is slightly softened, 8–10 minutes. Add 2 Tbsp. oil; season with salt and pepper. Toss to combine.
2. Place tuna in a medium bowl. Zest and juice lemon over tuna. Stir in 2 Tbsp. oil; season with salt and pepper.
3. Cut bread lengthwise without cutting all the way through. Add basil and parsley to olive mixture and toss to combine. Spread olive mixture over cut sides of baguette. Top with tuna, egg, tomato, and peppers, then drizzle with more oil; season with salt and pepper.
4. Wrap sandwich tightly in foil and weight down with a heavy skillet, 10 minutes. Cut in half before serving.

Easy Homemade Caesar Dressing

INGREDIENTS

- 3 oil-packed anchovy fillets, chopped
- 1 large garlic clove, chopped
- ¾ teaspoon (or more) kosher salt
- 1 large egg yolk
- 2 tablespoons fresh lemon juice
- ¾ teaspoon Dijon mustard
- ¼ cup plus 2 tablespoons vegetable oil
- 3 tablespoons Parmesan, finely grated

RECIPE PREPARATION

1. Mound anchovies, garlic, and salt on a cutting board. Using the side of a chef's knife, mash and chop until well combined, then continue to work mixture, holding knife blade at an angle, until a smooth paste forms. (Alternately, you can use a mortar and pestle or mini chopper to do this step.)
2. Whisk egg yolk, lemon juice, and mustard in a medium bowl. Place a kitchen towel in a medium saucepan, then place bowl in pan. (This holds the bowl in place while you whisk with one hand and pour oil with the other.)

3. Adding drop by drop to start and whisking constantly, drizzle a few drops of oil into yolk mixture. Continue, going slowly, until mixture looks slightly thickened and glossy. Continue to whisk, gradually adding oil in a slow, steady stream until all oil has been used and mixture looks like mayonnaise. Add a dash of water and whisk, adjusting with more water if needed, until dressing is the consistency of heavy cream. Add anchovy mixture and Parmesan and whisk until smooth. Taste and adjust seasoning with salt, if needed.

Linguine with Anchovies and Tuna
INGREDIENTS
- 5 tablespoons olive oil, divided
- 1 2-ounce tin oil-packed anchovies, chopped
- 6 garlic cloves, 5 sliced, 1 whole
- ½ teaspoon crushed red pepper flakes
- ¼ teaspoon smoked paprika
- 1 28-ounce can whole peeled tomatoes

- 1 bunch small Tuscan kale, ribs and stems removed
- Kosher salt
- 1 large slice stale sourdough or country-style bread, crusts removed, torn into 1-inch pieces
- ¼ cup finely chopped parsley
- 12 ounces linguine or other long strand pasta
- 1 6.7-ounce jar oil-packed tuna, drained

RECIPE PREPARATION

1. Heat 4 Tbsp. oil in a large skillet or pot over medium. Cook anchovies and sliced garlic, stirring occasionally, until anchovies are mostly dissolved and garlic is soft (do not let it brown), 6–8 minutes. Add red pepper flakes and paprika and cook, stirring, just until fragrant, about 30 seconds. Add tomatoes, crushing with your hands as you go. Break up with a wooden spoon until no large pieces remain; bring to a simmer and cook, stirring occasionally, until reduced to a very thick sauce, 20–25 minutes. Add a

splash of water to loosen; reduce heat to low and keep warm.

2. Meanwhile, blanch kale in a large pot of boiling salted water just until bright green, about 10 seconds. Transfer with a slotted spoon or tongs to a bowl of ice water; let cool. Drain and squeeze kale with your hands to remove excess water; coarsely chop. Reserve pot with kale cooking liquid for cooking pasta.

3. Pulse bread in a food processor until fine crumbs form. Toss breadcrumbs with remaining 1 Tbsp. oil in a medium skillet. Season with salt and gently toast over medium heat, tossing often, until golden brown and crunchy, 6–8 minutes. Finely grate remaining garlic clove over crumbs and stir to coat. Transfer to a small bowl and mix in parsley.

4. Bring kale cooking liquid to a boil and cook pasta, stirring occasionally, until al dente. Using tongs, transfer to skillet with sauce and

add kale and tuna. Toss to combine, adding water a few tablespoonfuls at a time to loosen as needed, until pasta is well coated. Serve pasta topped with breadcrumbs.

Saucy Chicken Puttanesca
INGREDIENTS
- 3 lb. skin-on, bone-in chicken thighs and drumsticks or whole legs
- Kosher salt
- 2 Tbsp. extra-virgin olive oil, plus more for drizzling
- 6 garlic cloves, thinly sliced
- 4 oil-packed anchovy fillets
- ½ tsp. crushed red pepper flakes
- 2 Tbsp. double-concentrated tomato paste
- 1 cup Castelvetrano olives, crushed, pits removed
- ¾ cup dry white wine
- 2 Tbsp. drained capers
- 2 fresh bay leaves (optional)

- 3 2" strips lemon peel, plus lemon wedges for serving

RECIPE PREPARATION

- Preheat oven to 350°. Pat chicken dry with paper towels, then season all over with salt.
- Heat 2 Tbsp. oil in a large skillet over medium-high until shimmering. Cook chicken, turning occasionally, until it has rendered some of its fat and skin is golden brown all over, 7–10 minutes. Transfer chicken to a plate. You'll have a pool of fat left in the pan. Spoon out all but 3 Tbsp. fat from pan. (Use it for roasted potatoes, in cooked bitter greens, or add to stewy beans.)
- Reduce heat to medium and add garlic and anchovies to skillet. Cook, stirring often, until garlic is softened and anchovies have disintegrated, 2–3 minutes. Sprinkle in red pepper flakes, then stir in tomato paste. Cook, stirring occasionally, until tomato paste begins to split and stick to pan, about 3 minutes. Add olives, wine, capers, bay leaves

- (if using), and lemon peel and bring to a simmer (still over medium heat). Cook, stirring occasionally, until most of the wine has evaporated, 5–7 minutes.
- Snuggle chicken (skin side up) into sauce in a single layer. Pour in 1 cup water and bring to a simmer. Transfer skillet to oven and bake, uncovered, until sauce is thickened and chicken is cooked through, 20–25 minutes (if using whole legs, it'll take closer to 30–35 minutes). Taste a spoonful of the sauce—it should be plenty salty between the anchovies and capers, so you most likely won't need to season with more salt.
- Transfer chicken to a platter and spoon sauce over. Drizzle with oil and serve with lemon wedges alongside.

Nasi Lemak
INGREDIENTS
Sambal Ikan Bilis

- 3½ oz. dried paper lantern chiles, dried bird chiles, or dried chiles de árbol
- 2 cups vegetable oil
- ½ cup red-skin Spanish peanuts
- 2½ cups small dried anchovies
- 2 medium shallots, halved
- 3 garlic cloves
- 2 Holland chiles, stems removed, halved lengthwise
- 4½ tsp. sugar
- 1½ tsp. tamarind concentrate

Rice and Assembly

- 2 cups jasmine rice
- 1 tsp. kosher salt
- 3 pandan leaves (optional)
- ½ cup light unsweetened coconut milk
- 4 large eggs
- ½ English hothouse cucumber, cut in half lengthwise, thinly sliced crosswise
- Soy sauce (for serving)

Ingredient Info

- Paper lantern chiles can be found at Asian markets and themalamarket.com. Tamarind concentrate, often labeled "concentrate cooking tamarind," can be found at Asian and Thai markets.

RECIPE PREPARATION

Sambal Ikan Bilis

1. Chop paper lantern chiles into ½" pieces, discarding most of the seeds that fall out. Place in a small bowl and pour in boiling water to cover. Let sit 30 minutes to soften, then drain.

2. Meanwhile, bring oil and peanuts to a gentle simmer in a small saucepan over medium heat; cook, adjusting heat as needed, until peanuts are golden brown, 6–8 minutes. Using a slotted spoon, transfer nuts to paper towels to drain; set aside for serving. Immediately add anchovies to oil and cook until golden brown and crisp, about 2 minutes. Transfer to fresh paper towels; let cool. Set ¼ cup oil aside.

3. Pulse shallots, garlic, and ¼ cup fried anchovies (save remaining anchovies for serving) in a food processor until a smooth paste forms. Transfer to a medium bowl. Add paper lantern and Holland chiles to food processor (no need to clean) and pulse until very smooth and no visible pieces of dried chile remain. Transfer chile purée to a small bowl.
4. Heat reserved oil in a medium skillet over medium-high until shimmering. Add shallot mixture and cook, stirring, until slightly darkened in color and fragrant, about 2 minutes. Mix in chile purée and cook, stirring often, until it starts to stick to bottom of skillet, about 3 minutes. Reduce heat to low. Add sugar, tamarind concentrate, and ¼ cup water and cook, stirring often, until sambal is much darker in color and thickened, 25–35 minutes.
5. Do Ahead: Sambal ikan bilis can be made 1 week ahead. Let cool; cover and chill.

Rice and Assembly

6. Place rice in a medium saucepan and pour in cold water to cover; swirl with your hands to rinse away some of the starch. Drain and repeat process 2 more times. Water should be just slightly cloudy at this point. Place rinsed rice back into saucepan and cover with 2½ cups cold water; stir in salt. Gather pandan leaves (if using) together and tie into a knot; add to pan. Bring rice to a simmer over medium-high heat. Cover pan and reduce heat to low; cook 18 minutes. Remove lid and stir in coconut milk. Cover, remove from heat, and let sit 5 minutes.

7. Meanwhile, bring a small saucepan of water to a boil. Carefully lower eggs into water. Cook 10 minutes, then transfer to a bowl of ice water and let cool. Peel eggs and cut in half lengthwise.

8. Combine sambal ikan bilis, reserved fried peanuts, and reserved fried anchovies in a medium bowl and toss to evenly coat. Scoop

a generous ½ cup sambal mixture into a 12-oz. bowl. Top with 1½ cups rice and pack into bowl with a rubber spatula to compress. The bowl should be filled to the rim. Place a slightly larger bowl upside down over bowl of rice. Invert so larger bowl is now on the bottom; lift off smaller bowl. You should have a dome of rice and anchovy mixture nestled in the center of the larger bowl. Arrange 8 cucumber slices around rice dome, overlapping slightly to make a semicircle. Add 2 egg halves to side of rice with no cucumber slices; season yolks lightly with soy sauce. Repeat with remaining rice, sambal mixture, cucumbers, and eggs to make 3 more bowls.

Linguine with Green Olive Sauce and Zesty Breadcrumbs

INGREDIENTS
- 1 tablespoon plus ½ cup olive oil
- ¼ cup panko (Japanese breadcrumbs)
- Kosher salt and freshly ground black pepper
- 2 tablespoons chopped fresh dill
- 1 teaspoon finely grated lemon zest
- 12 ounces linguine or other long pasta
- 4 oil-packed anchovy fillets
- 1 small garlic clove
- 1 cup chopped fresh parsley
- ½ cup chopped fresh basil
- 1 cup green olives, pitted, halved
- 3 tablespoons drained capers
- ½ ounce Parmesan, finely grated (about ½ cup), plus more for serving
- 2 tablespoons fresh lemon juice

RECIPE PREPARATION
1. Heat 1 Tbsp. oil in a medium skillet over medium and cook panko, stirring, until golden, about 5 minutes. Season with salt and

pepper; transfer to paper towels to drain and toss with dill and lemon zest.

2. Cook pasta in a large pot of boiling salted water, stirring occasionally, until al dente. Drain, reserving ½ cup pasta cooking liquid.
3. Meanwhile, mash anchovies and garlic to a paste on a cutting board with the side of a chef's knife. Combine with parsley, basil, and half of olives and capers in a large bowl. Chop remaining olives and capers and add to bowl, along with remaining ½ cup oil. Mix well; season sauce with salt and pepper.
4. Add pasta and ¼ cup reserved pasta cooking liquid to sauce. Toss, adding Parmesan a bit at a time, along with more pasta cooking liquid as needed, until sauce coats pasta. Add lemon juice; season with salt and pepper.
5. Serve pasta topped with panko and more Parmesan.
6. Do Ahead: Sauce can be made 1 day ahead. Cover with plastic wrap, pressing directly against surface, and chill.

Escarole Salad with Anchovy Cream and Crispy Quinoa

INGREDIENTS

- ¼ cup red or white quinoa
- Kosher salt
- Vegetable oil (for frying; about 1 cup)
- 6 oil-packed anchovy fillets, chopped
- 1 garlic clove, chopped
- ⅓ cup heavy cream
- 2 teaspoons apple cider vinegar
- 2 teaspoons Dijon mustard
- ½ teaspoon honey
- 6 cups torn escarole (from about 2 small heads)
- ½ cup mixed herb leaves (such as parsley and/or dill)
- Freshly ground black pepper
- Shaved Parmesan (for serving)

RECIPE PREPARATION

1. Cook quinoa in a small pot of boiling salted water until tender, 10–15 minutes. Drain and

transfer to a paper towel–lined rimmed baked sheet. Let sit, tossing occasionally, until dry, 20–25 minutes.

2. Pour oil to come ¼" up the sides of a medium skillet; heat over medium-high. Fry quinoa, stirring occasionally, until sizzling subsides, about 3 minutes. Transfer to paper towels to drain.
3. Place anchovies, garlic, and a pinch of salt on a cutting board. Using the side of a chef's knife, smash anchovies and garlic into a paste (this can also be done in a mortar and pestle). Transfer paste to a medium bowl and whisk in cream, vinegar, mustard, and honey.
4. Add escarole and herbs to anchovy cream; season with salt and pepper and toss to combine.
5. Serve salad topped with fried quinoa and Parmesan.
6. Do Ahead: Quinoa can be fried 1 day ahead; store airtight at room temperature. Anchovy

cream can be made 1 day ahead; cover and chill.

CONCLUSION

Gastroparesis is either temporary or chronic. It can be a symptom of another condition, or it can be idiopathic, which means the cause is unknown. No matter what the cause or duration of your gastroparesis, eating small meals and limiting your fiber and fat intake can help your digestion.

Different people with different diagnoses can tolerate certain food items better than others. Always speak with your doctor about your individualized nutritional needs while treating gastroparesis.

It's important to make sure that your body is still getting the vitamins and minerals necessary for healthy organ function as you recover from your gastroparesis symptoms.

The gastroparesis diet is always the first step to treating this condition after diagnosis. The easy-to-digest foods it promotes put less stress on your gastrointestinal system, reducing a range of uncomfortable symptoms such as nausea, vomiting, acid reflux, bloating, and abdominal pain.

Furthermore, the focus on nutrient density helps your body weather bouts of appetite loss that often arise during flare-ups. Without a consistent focus on good nutrition, these episodes could lead to malnutrition and weight loss.

Following a gastroparesis diet may also help you avoid medications and other treatments for the condition that may be associated with side effects.

Studies investigating specific foods to consume and foods to avoid on a gastroparesis diet were lacking until 2015. In fact, according to a 2016 report published in Clinical Gastroenterology and Hepatology, patients traditionally received dietary advice based on physiological principles rather than scientific evidence.

However, more recent clinical trials have identified specific foods and food characteristics that help improve the comfort level of those living with gastroparesis.

For example, one study published in Digestive Diseases and Sciencessought out to identify and characterize specific foods that affect gastroparesis. Based on patient experiences, researchers were able to compile a list of foods that changed participants' symptoms.

Foods that provoked symptoms were usually acidic, fatty, spicy, or roughage-based. Tolerable foods were usually bitter, salty, bland, and sweet.

There is no cure for gastroparesis. Dietary changes and other treatments (including medications and other options) can help you manage the symptoms. Therefore, you should plan to adopt the gastroparesis diet for the long-term.

CPSIA information can be obtained
at www.ICGtesting.com
Printed in the USA
LVHW040158240223
740335LV00015B/844